Praise

Beauty lies in truth, hardcore, from the depths of the soul. Jacqueline Cioffa' takes us there, brave, raw & unfiltered.

—Sandra Bernhard

A call to arms for women of all ages, author Jacqueline Cioffa has sheathed the collective force of the divine feminine. Her transcendent poetry collection "The Shape of Us" gracefully carries the reader through the valley of despair to the peak of triumph. Offering the wounded a voice, encouraging the tentative with conviction, Cioffa's medley from the heart is victorious in its rendering. A must-read for generations to come, "The Shape of Us", arouses the spirit of survival, it is a tribal war cry. Being a woman, celebrated for our multi-facets as Cioffa extolls never felt so good. Bravo!

—Julie Anderson
Supermodel, Founder of Feminine Collective
Love Notes From Humanity, and *Raw and Unfiltered* anthologies,
Secrets and Lies, Author

Jackie Cioffa has bestowed upon women a gift that is for each stage of their lives. The Shape of Us is for the mothers with daughters as well as daughters with mothers—a complicated relationship fraught with intertwined expectations that can never be fulfilled no matter how much they are hoped for. Cioffa's poetry is for the images in our mirrors that don't match up to the societal expectations that have impregnated themselves in our self-worth, bearing the fruit of self-loathing. There are presents for the strong women who know what it means to be afraid of love because they've never known it to be kind. The Shape of Us is meant for the survivors, all of us who have secreted away dark memories that we won't allow to define our lives.

Yes, The Shape of Us is a gift, though Cioffa reminds her readers that they "are the happy accidental gift, dying since way before birth" (Gravity). And isn't a miracle that all of us are so alive? In all of our shapes and stages, we are women to be celebrated, and Cioffa's poetry and prose accomplishes this.

—C. Streetlights
Black Sheep, Rising, Author

As a fellow columnist on Feminine Collective, I have long admired the poetry, fiction, and inspiring work written by Jacqueline Cioffa. Her column, Bleeding Ink, is a compelling read traveling from poetry and prose to narrative essays offering original observations on the human condition. Cioffa wrote two engrossing fiction books in The Vast Landscape *and* Georgia Pine *saga. I fell in love with her relatable protagonist Harrison who bore semi-autobiographical traits of the author. I fell in love all over again when she wrote* The Red Bench. *This memoir spoke to me on a personal level as I, too, have battled the diagnosis of manic depression and have spiraled in and out of the madness of this disease. I eagerly await the release of her new book,* The Shape of Us, *a collection of writings doing what Cioffa does best—celebrating women, whose collective voices she hears, acknowledges, and answers. Over decades of life as an international model, celebrity makeup artist, author and poet, she has gathered every valuable happiness, sorrow, self-reflection, and lessons learned into a mellifluous melody of lessons shared. Cioffa is a powerful voice of the decade and* The Shape of Us *illustrates her significant impact on women everywhere longing to be understood and heard. Brava to Cioffa for another gift to her followers.*

—Dori Owen
Feminine Collective columnist, contributing poet and author to *Love Notes From Humanity, You Are Not Your Rape* anthology, and *Raw & Unfiltered.* Essayist published in The Mighty, The Lithium Chronicles, Stigma Fighters, OTV Magazine, and the literary mag Sudden Denouement.

The moment I finished reading the Shape of Us, I felt a tremendous sense of gratitude to Jackie Cioffa for gifting us with this stunning work of literary art. An exquisite experience causing gorgeous tears to roll down my cheeks intermingled with smiles and nods of agreement. The Shape of Us is for everyone. Jackie speaks to the beauty, wonder, magic, trials and challenges of being a woman but also speaks to the human journey which is represented on the pages offering men a better understanding of the female experience...the inner and outer struggles. Joy and sadness. Love and loss. Beauty and ugliness. Motherhood and sisterhood. I will read this beautiful book again and again. It will be a gift to all the women in my life who have touched me in some way and an offering of love to those who need a place to go to reconnect with their inner warrior goddess.

Cioffa dares to once again share the magic and majesty of her words. To paint a picture on the page that can only be seen in the mind of the reader...their own personal journey inspired through her poetic expression.

—Amalia Natalio
Founder of
KarmicKindness & The Sacred Sisterhood Movement

When I read Jackie's poems, I'm transported back to a time when I was also insecure and trying to figure out my role in this world. And as a mother of young adults, I feel a bit more connected to them.

– Mary Rowen,
Leaving the Beach, Living by Ear, Author

The magic of Cioffa's work shines its light on the power of the written word.

—Julie Davidow, American Contemporary Artist,
co-author of Miami Contemporary Artists

I was always impressed by how courageous a writer Jacqueline is. Keep writing your fine prose.

—Mark Blickley,
Sacred Misfits, Dream Streams, a text-based art book, and *Weathered Reports: Trump Surrogate Quotes from the Underground*, Author and Playwright

Praise for Jacqueline's Books

In The Red Bench, *Jacqueline Cioffa provides a raw, real and painfully honest description of her battles with bipolar disorder. As a clinical psychologist, I have had years of experience as a mental health provider and as an advocate. I can say with assurance that* The Red Bench *is perhaps the most eloquent first-person account of mental illness I have ever read. Cioffa's narrative is both lyrical and disturbing, showing the full burden of her struggle, while also offering hope and inspiration for brighter days to come.*

—David T. Susman, PhD

Jaqueline Cioffa writes with such a soul-stirring intensity that it can't help but ignite a passion in her readers. I took my time with this book, and I loved every single moment of it. Harrison is beautiful in her strength and vulnerability. She spoke to me in ways that a character never has. The Vast Landscape is both beautifully written, and deeply meaningful.

—Nicole Lyons
Bestselling author of *The Lithium Chronicles,*

Beautifully written, author Jackie Cioffa masters one of the cardinal rules of storytelling, know your characters mentally, physically, and emotionally. Cioffa nails it in this fantastic sequel to The Vast Landscape, *by not only drawing the reader into the mind of the central character, but also eliciting heartfelt emotions from the reader as the lives of the characters unfold. Readers of* The Vast Landscape *will love this continuation. It left me anxiously anticipating another story in the series.*

—John E. Crowther,
author/ creator of the acclaimed
Comic Book Series, *Rochelle*

The Shape of Us

Jacqueline Cioffa

Selected poems and essays
Copyright © 2019 by Jacqueline Cioffa

All rights reserved. No part of this book may be reproduced or used in any manner without written permission of the copyright owner except for the use of quotations in a book review.

FIRST EDITION

ISBN 9781706531418

Book Interior Design & eBook Adaptation: Deena Rae; E-BookBuilders

Independently Published
www.jacquelinecioffa.com

books by jacqueline

The Red Bench
The Vast Landscape
Georgia Pine

Contents

books by jacqueline i
dedication .... m
women who shape us 1
sweet child of mine 3
white boots and freckled faces 6
barely a girl 8
gravity 13
hey now, girl 15
fancy pajamas at high noon 20
becoming 21
buh, bye 22
all i ever wanted 23
big girls wear boxers 27
looking glass and the windowpane 28
yogafide 30
female persuasion 33
embers and ash 35
don't call me daughter 37
the inheritance tax 43
faded glory 47
little black dress 48
the highway halfway mark 49
vainglorious 51
beautiful you 52
girl in progress 53
luck be a lady 54
stomping ground 55
yes mother 63
against the current 65
the shadow of her grace 66
corsets and candy 73
you're a knockout 74

k

mother, may i 77
sky's no limit 81
toxic lady 82
sister of my soul 84
in between the rain 88
my first bff, and forever friend 93
my body, my choice 95
dance party 99
if the shoe fits 103
bad bitches 104
gum on your shoe 105
beauty reigns optimistic 106
hello, dolly 107
my girl gone missing 108
radical acceptance 110
to know the love of a good man 113
acknowledgements 115
about the author 119

dedication

Dedicated to all the glorious, gorgeous, empowered sisters of my soul. The survivors, rebels, outcasts, lightning rods, and quiet heroines.

For the tough as nails warrior women, I have adored, aspired, and admired.

You have made me feel worthy of the sweet, soft miracle it is to be born a girl, in these fast and loud, masculine modern times.

THE SHAPE OF US

women who shape us

She won't hesitate to call out a bully, misanthrope or liar
She will stand tall, pull her shoulders back while sobbing, heaving hysterical for the plight of another
She'll dance crazed and belt out a tune just to hear the stereo beat and guitar riffs and drum solo
She will love a man or a woman on a whim from a sweet smile and soft whispers
She's unafraid to get broken
Her brokenness owned by the cracks she boldly dared step upon walking chin up towards the sun
Pride, she'll swallow it every time for a cause
And a saving grace melody
She wears leather or lace
And loves to play dress up
She needs to look pretty not for others
Nah, man
For her glorious, unique, mysterious self
Because she is all woman, all day
And one of a kind
Clever, neat, messy and soulful
She's not a feminist
She's a humanist who happens to be a girl
In love with this one life even when it hurts

...becoming

sweet child of mine

My darling child how would you like to be? The paper is yet a seed and not even a tree. Its star stuff swirling about, twisting, turning, churning, clashing and recycling waiting on you. It's all yours, this one life you've yet to live. The molecular, cellular neurons of infinite possibility are bubbling and bursting with frenetic energy. Don't you fret about the Science; I've got that worked out. Sweet child of light and love and mystery map it out. Go ahead, the perfect spontaneous combustion of blood, thinking mind and oxygen.

Anything? Really? I can be any old which way I want? Wow. That's a whole lot of responsibility. Okay, let me think. Just for a short little teeny smidgen while. Let me stay in my transparent, weightless, formless white bouncing bubble. The orbs are so beautiful up here, heaven consists of white, transparent bubbles in varying sizes, forever moving and colliding in the stratosphere.

No, no my darling don't overthink it; don't try too hard.

Okay, I think I understand. I get a full size, funky groovy physical body and a freewheeling willful thoughtful attentive mind?

Yes, exactly like that. You're getting it now, it's not yours forever so be sure to make the stark-naked birthday suit snug with plenty of room to grow.

Ooh goody. I'd like to be lovely, wanted and kind. I'd like to feel happy, funny and proud. Make me loyal and true, surrounded by humans who adore my company. Ooh ooh ooh yes, I'd like that very much to be likeable. That matters, right? I'd want to be brave, adventurous, scale majestic mountains and feel the wind coursing cold through my veins while tickling the leaves on the trees. You know, really know the climate, experience the burn and sweat and chills. I want to feel it all; Freestyle, lightning, thunder, carnival, cotton candy sticky sappy drippy love, music and melody. I want to float, weightless. Make me loud and quiet, clear and crazy buoyant alive. I'd like to swim naked twisting and smiling, dance without rhyme and sing off-key. And giggle you know and laugh, like a lot. I'd want to worship my time. I'd like to be remembered by the etchings in towering ancient bamboo stalks. I'd like to be remembered by how much I loved being, alive.

Is that all of it, you think?

No, no, no. Almost. I want to know endless wine-dark seas, mystery and spend time in an open transparent glass house. I want to hear riptide waves of emotion crashing off the sea. I suppose I want it all. Make me pretty, pretty pretty please. Pretty inside with honesty exploding through my pores.

Is that everything? Are you sure?

Oh no. Hold on, wait one tiny second let me dream a little bit further, bigger, wider. More sky, more stars, more fire, more water, more spontaneous, and more of everything ignition.

Make me a colorful palette of emotions.
Make me a colorful palette of emotions.
I DON'T CARE.

I won't remember being alive, being human anyway. Will I?

No, no, no! I'm going… ready or not. It'll be over before I can take in and fully grasp one human breath. Maybe you could add a pause button, please, so I might be more than some other being's fading memory? Perhaps I can stay down there, just a little while longer? Not forever, no, I know. I understand. Just long enough, enough time so I can get it. Get what this living thing is about. Please, please, pretty please?

I really, really, really want to go. I think I've got it all mapped out.

Oh, sweet child, sweet child of mine.
You're ready, now. Just go live it.

Okay. I'm almost ready.
One last very, very important thing?

Make me a girl.

white boots and freckled faces

Where is the child?
Where has she gone?
Did she get bruised and beaten down?
Oh she's there
Over there
There she is
Dancing and laughing
And spinning
Wide-open
She still believes in a better place
And a better time
And sees the good in mankind
Muddled behind the murky water
And she cries a real tear
One teardrop
For all that is gone
And counts
And she gets it
And sometimes she wants to die
So swollen with emotion
Not afraid to cry
Not afraid to be touched
She doesn't cringe at the thought of physical intimacy
And she's full of trust
And she's let go of the void
She's the voyeur, the mighty, the strong

The Shape of Us

She's her mother and father and brothers *and sisters*
All rolled into this neat package
That's the best of all of them

barely a girl

To steal all that was pure and innocent
Before she had the chance to experience
All the changing shapes of her body
The first kiss, crush, giddiness, and her exploding sexuality
Making her feel dirty and ashamed
Carrying secrets that did not belong to her
Not yet a woman, barely a girl, and merely a child
Undressed and exposed
A child who would grow up and cower by the touch of physical intimacy
A tender hug sending her spiraling and years spent in therapy
To release the shame and blame
It would take a long time, patience, and slow healing
Before terror and self-doubt turned into a firm no
And solid boundaries
The blossoming girl
Unable and unwilling to celebrate her sexuality
Her innocence lost under baggy clothing
It would take many years and tears
Before the triggers turned into recovery
Her body strong
Reclaiming her feminine beauty long after the abuse, trauma, and insecurity
To the sick men unworthy of her forgiveness
She must forgive them anyway

She understands
In spite of her trembling skin and naked insecurity

To let go of the secret, take her time becoming kind with herself
Healing all the broken parts
The disgusting, immoral monsters are not good men, but evil and small
They are the only ones to shoulder the blame
Stop allowing vile, perverted, powerful men to hide
Behind lies and excuses
They are morally and wholly responsible
You're safe now
Call them out
Young girl on the cusp of becoming
I'm proud to stand shoulder to shoulder with you
Feminine divine
No child must ever feel unprotected or dirty or not believed
I believe you
We believe you
It's okay
You're safe now
To forgive, but never forget to carry on
The heavy burden, shrouded in secrecy is not yours to bear
You were not a woman, just barely a girl and merely a child
Soft and tender, on the cusp of womanhood and sexual discovery

You, sweet child of mine
Did absolutely nothing wrong
Forgive me while a cry awhile
For innocence lost
Until I am goddamn good and ready
To rise up
One woman scorned, abused, and violated hurts us all
Together we fight
Against all that is ugly and inexcusably wrong

No longer a girl, or merely a child
But grown women now
Willing and able to stand our ground
For all the girls, and boys who live scared, shamed into silence

Jacqueline Cioffa

Ending this vicious cycle of abuse right here, right now
What do you see when you see a child who's barely a girl?
Now picture she's your daughter, wholesome and pure
Worthy
Protected by an army of good men
Sadly, this fucked up society is not there for her
Until then, we got you
No longer a child or barely a girl but soldiers
A band of fierce females and wolfpack women
Whose voices no longer shake but carry yours too

Do not doubt for one second I don't see your worth. Your quiet blush soul shines bright, and without fanfare. More real, more sensitive, more human than any crumbling Hollywood star. You're solid, liquid gold like the pavements you pound underfoot. Dreaming is free, when you're brave enough to dance, pretty in pink.

gravity

Silly girl, your dreams will become quieter with age but never less full.

All the colors are yours to suit your mood.

I love you colorblind, and the blackest of Neptune's blues.

You are prettier than the atmosphere three billion light-years forgotten from here.

I will whisper in your ear when you're fast asleep to always, always care.

To emote, to feel, to share.

To gift away love.

To gift away only love, while dreaming as bold and big as you dare.

I hope you always, always care more.

Never, ever less.

No matter the cost.

Or the climate.

Living is pretty even when it hurts.

You are loved because of your flaws, more than rainbows, puppies, unicorns and silly human things.

I am gravity and I am here to help you stay grounded to the earth.

You are the cosmic miracle of constellations and suns and moons colliding and exploding in the stratosphere.

Jacqueline Cioffa

You are the happy accidental gift, dying since way before birth.

hey now, girl

Hey now, girl
Don't clench your fists when you walk down the street
Please, just don't
Don't look down and hide your pretty face
Smile at a stranger with your arms open wide

Hey now, girl
Don't be naïve
Not everyone sees your sweet, innocent intentions
Or notices your inquisitive eyes in the most, appropriate meaningful way
Be curiously cautious
You were not taught to cower
You were not taught to slouch your shoulders in shame
You learned all that
And unlearned it
You were taught to soar
To twirl in place
Dizzily kicking your feet all giggly as you fell to the floor

Hey now, girl
How are those rain puddles?
Do they annoy the shit out of you or make you smile mischievous?
Do you jump smack dab in the middle your feet soaking wet
Chuckling through the gap in your teeth and sopping rain gear

Hey, now girl
You don't get a rewind button, forge ahead
Do you hastily walk around the puddle nuisance bumping head on into pedestrians?

Jacqueline Cioffa

Hey now, girl
Silly girl, let your glorious long locks fly into the wind
Do not tie them back into an uptight, neat bun
No, no do not, do not do that

Hey now, girl
Precious one
Why are you wiping the tears from your flushed cheeks
Embarrassed
Let them fall freely
The beautiful, stunning cascades of vulnerability
Wear your emotions on your tight, muscular biceps
Let it bleed
Your heart for humanity now and again

Hey now, girl
Let the rivers guide you upstream
Do not take the easiest path, the downstream one, or listen to loose propaganda
Pay no mind
To the bullies at school, the mean girls who dubbed you little freak

Hey now, girl
Don't you fret or remember their vitriol with spite or regret
You were the individual way back when
Shrug it off with a glass of Chardonnay and a wink
Hey now, funky girl with the wide-eyed rims, purple highlights and beat up Nikes
You shone metallic with silver wings on the soles of your feet
And disco balls above your head

Hey now, girl
Shrug your shoulders at the ignorant boys to men who made you cry
They did not understand your superhero powers

Hey now, girl
You grew solid, strong and mighty
With golden specks of fire coursing through your veins

The Shape of Us

You wouldn't wait for any man to mend a broken heart
Nah, you'd smile and swim upstream because the currents felt good and fresh
Inviting and cold
Alive

Hey now, girl
It took a whole lot of time and patience to get here
Free from the blame, shame, fear, and guilt game
Society plays tricks on naïve, youngins'
Creating creepy, crafty adults

Hey now, girl
Eat vanilla ice cream dripping with hot fudge; mountains of whip cream and three cherries on top
Dance and wave your arms up and out without a care
Sing out of tune; belt the words like it's your last five seconds of breath
Laugh without bringing your hands up to cover your mouth
Laugh loud, proud and often
Cry rivers and rivers of tears
Tidal waves of love, hope, faith, and devotion

Hey now, girl
You are going to be A- OKAY
You are going to be just fine and dandy
On your own
Don't wait for tomorrow to watch the sunrise over the equator
To feel the muscles in your legs strong and tight as you hike
Miracle mountains of trouble and strife

Hey now, girl
'Cuss like a boy
Go ahead, say FUCK YOU whenever appropriate and as often as you like

Hey now, girl
Hush now
Don't waste your foul mouth resentment, bitter aftertaste or hate on

the haters, fear mongrels, or naysayers
The ones who don't see you
I do
You do too
Ladies can't help but feel in sync

Hey now, girl
I see the strut and double time tap in your foot

Hey now, girl
I've seen through the walls that people tried to build around you
You kicked them down, brick by brick

Hey now, girl
You are your mothers and mothers and mothers' daughter
Strong, confident and able
Unclench those fists and do the work
There is tilling to be done
Freedom, faith, hope and resolution to be reborn
Under the seedlings of the majestic oak
And the concrete towers and city streets
Ghetto fabulous, you are adaptable and oh so lovely
When
You lead with human kindness, empathy, and understanding
I get excited all over again
At the possibility

Hey now, girl
You're all grown up
Into the most glorious, statuesque, creation
You are woman, now
Go on
And get it
You, role model
Show us proud
To shout, 'hey now, girl'
Into the future

Hey now, girl

You can be anything you want, anything at all
You are the prettiest child, the blank slate young face

Hey now, girls
You are the next generation, the future dreamers, puddle jumpers and doers
The dancers
Of beautiful determination
Together
We stand proud

fancy pajamas at high noon

If you're tired, I will sit with you.
When you're stressed, I'll bring pink balloons and Bazooka bubble gum.

When your heart is broken, I'll make you a killer playlist with all your favorite tunes.
When you're down, I'll nod and listen.
Because most every shitty scenario.

I've been there too.
What I won't ever do is lie and tell you everything will get better real soon.

Who the hell knows when, but it will.
With a little bit of patience, luck and timing.
It might not be tomorrow, but someday real soon you'll grow tired of wearing fancy pajamas at noon.
You'll never live up to your ridiculously high expectations.
Stop beating yourself up, comparing, judging, berating.
I see your beauty hidden beneath the diamonds and pearls.
You are amazingly, spectacularly, fantastically funny enough.
I'm here to tell you it's okay we all get buried by the bullshit and the noise.

Just get up.

becoming

Beautiful resides behind the twinkling eyes of adolescent curiosity and bursting womanhood. True beauty lives inside the laugh lines, tears, scars, vulnerability, and mystery we carry, while holding our heads held high.

To appreciate and admire the feminine mystique, her strength, bursting curves, quirks, and perfect imperfections.

Beauty is your birthright, face, mind and body.

It's the soft, gentle and proud way you carry yourself after a storm, and the sunshine you gracefully left behind.

Do not cower. Do not hide. Do not doubt.

Show up, every single time.

You are the whole package.

buh, bye

You were the storm in my soul
My midnight moon, and personal tsunami
Liquid angst
To love you
To know I really loved you
Quietly and with a certain steadfastness
Twenty years full and counting
That's really something

…hold up

I've changed my mind
I'm tired of waiting to be seen
For all the beauty I bestow
The who I truly am
I'm not holding out for a hero
I'm becoming
My very own one and only, loyal and true
Crazy diamond
Independent and whole
Without you

all i ever wanted

All I ever wanted was for you to be happy.
Without the clothes, the bling, the boys, all the heavy stuff.
To be deliriously happy without watching the tick-tock of the clock, afraid that your time for bliss had past.
It has not.
You deserve to feel joy, wonder, love and laughter until your heart beat's quiet.
All I ever wanted was to see you smile wide and large, for you to feel the beats of your most favorite, carefree, wild and meaningful dance songs.
All I ever wanted was to make you a joyful and triumphant playlist to drown out the bullshit, the chatter and the background noise.
All I ever wanted was for you to forget about the world and her woes for a minute, and dance around in your big girl briefs out of the shadows and away from the dark.
Alone, and A-Okay on your own, little darlin.'
Happiness is allowed and encouraged, it's alright to wear your pain on the inside out, like an armor of loud love.
The gospel choir sings and claps jubilee come Sunday afternoon.
You can't help yourself, you join in, a little lighter than yesterday.
There's collective faith vibrating in the room.
You and you and you and me, right here and now, feeling free and a hint of happy, touching your fingers while tapping your toes.
Don't ever let go of the soundtrack of a kind life that fills your heart and replenishes the soul.

I exist; therefore, I am, beautifully flawed strength, smiles and bravado. I don't want to be considered just a girl. I want to be remembered as a kind, master student of life and art. An honest girl, warrior woman, and fellow sister traveler, leading with rainbow hues of courage shooting stars straight from the heart.

big girls wear boxers

Boys will come and go
But your big girl heart
will only continue to grow
Creating fields of stilettos and spunk
Your broken heart magically mends
dancing mischievous
Adventurous and whole
Boys may come and go
But not your girls, sisters, partners in crime
They will never leave you eating dime store cowgirl chocolates alone
They'll bring 24 carat diamonds of hope
Sexy silliness and laughter to your lips
Toasting to no regrets and moving on
To your tough as nails, sweet, messy,
vulnerable, cussing, mysterious, warrior queen
Unapologetic female self
With pitchers of margaritas, tacos, sassiness and zero guilt

looking glass and the windowpane

Let's face it; there's no fooling. The sagging skin, the wrinkled face, the ridiculous forty something woman in short skirts and bottled-up Botox. The gravitational pull and the eventual flight back home were booked in advance. You already hold the winning ticket. I recognize the faces in the street, the fear, the familiar grimace and disgust at the sideways glance in the shop's windowpane. I see the doubt, the two-second pause, the roll of the eyes in the rearview mirror. I'm going to rise above it, be the lady lit from within. I'm going to honor this body that works, that walks me from place to place. I'm going to love this heart that beats and eyes that see the sun and feel the heat, and arms that sway to the rhythm and ears that hear the beat. I'm going to resist the tug; I'm going to dig the features and the sum. I'm going to take the very best care. Every so often, I'm going to eat eggs with buttered toast and pancakes dripping in maple syrup. I'm going to drink beer without the guilt. I'm going to love a man head on without flipping the light. Sooner or later, I'm going to want to play the parts. I'll be mother, daughter, sister, lover, and feminist right on time. I'll want to write the appropriate words that answer the meaningful questions. I'll get the joke. I'll laugh out loud without bringing my hands up to cover my face. I am timeless, ageless and the perfect temperature. I will not grimace at the sight of a beautiful young woman. I will nod and offer her a secret, knowing smile and familiar glance. I will put away the minis, the boots, and the crazy forms of self-expression and store them deep in the back of my closet. I'll hold onto them for a younger version of myself. I no longer have any use. I'll walk the walk with conviction. I'll talk the talk and hear the discussion. I will listen, with a mind that is open. I will wait ten seconds to answer. I'll have a well-thought out appropriate response. I'll take an interest in the world around me. I'll be empowered, insightful, bright and impulsive in an instant. I will mellow out and leave fear, jealousy and rage behind. I'll do all the things that a grown up does. I will act like a curvy, sophisticated, well-groomed woman. I will see the face and body; I will embrace and endorse the beautiful. I will tuck away my first-class ticket in the back pocket of my favorite pair of ripped, familiar blue jeans for a later date. I will remember where I put it. I'll keep my head on straight, high upon my strong, beautiful shoulders. I will put one determined foot in front of the other. For now, I'm just going to walk. And face the window without the pain.

yogafide

To the girls who rule the art of downward dog, plank position, discipline, giggles, breath, chitchat, patience, practice, and friendship. You are my blessed, sacred, and capable sunshine, my beautiful afternoon tribe.

"She prays cruelty learns from compassion. She hopes time has made earth a softer, more malleable place to visit. Shame and fear obliterated; life colored with happy minutes."
— The Vast Landscape

female persuasion

Don't worry if they don't like you, worry when you despise yourself. In a world where you're taught that pretty fits inside some prefabricated box, grab some scissors and create your own unique shape, one that you're most comfortable in. Leave room for growth and femininity, as you navigate the highs and lows. Do not cower, quiver or apologize for being a strong woman with a voice, dream and vision. Do not change because someone makes you feel dirty or uncomfortable with the way you dress, wear your hair, or the sky-high pink stilettos you pair with a camouflage skirt. Personally, I prefer some kicking ass and taking names combat boots. In time you'll learn to sit silently with your body in a crowded room without flinching, self-confidence your trusted companion.

The gut will never lie, abuse or desert you. Nor will the truth. It won't always be easy, the arduous journey or the various compromises being a woman presents. It won't always be easy loving yourself. It'll be hard, and there will be mountains of shame and self-doubt. You're only human, girlfriend. Be authentically you. The you that has earned a well-educated, thoughtful, and respected opinion is your sexiest asset. Be kind, but firm and take nobody's bullshit. When a man tries to violate your sacred body, or whistles when you walk past, you have the absolute right to say nope, not today, not ever. And, fuck you. To the fathers and mothers who raise decent, respectful daughters and sons, I commend you.

To the fathers, mothers and others who enable cowards, perverts and predators, I say fuck you.

Fuck you for excusing disgusting behavior, and locker room banter bullshit. You, beautiful girl, did nothing wrong. Never apologize for being the lady you are, or the awkward young girl still becoming. Every single time a woman annihilates Pandora's square box concealed with lies, abuse, rocks and shame, she frees others to do the same. You are worthy, and your story does not end with blame or shame. It begins anew, her body and innocence, reclaimed.

embers and ash

Oh dear, have you seen her?
She was right here a minute ago. I swear. I can still smell her cheap $5.00 perfume and tobacco trail. I didn't know. I was ill-prepared, unfit for this thing called a lifespan. How to navigate the hillbilly, redneck back roads without a compass of one's own?
Abandoned, sidetracked, lost in the strange moments rolled into one. Bone crushing, blood pulsing, cotton candy sticky, all-consuming love. I have not been on the other side; I do not know how she feels. I did not experience the pain of giving birth, the miracle of a helpless creature cradled in her arms, heart to heart beating.
To feel precisely how she feels I cannot know.
I am out of my depth, in foreign waters. The grown-up child still needs her, close. The mere presence calms the rattled, shaky, knee scraped bones. I could never be that good. Selfless, compassionate, proud to mop floors, cook dinners, wash clothes and carry heavy loads without fuss. A lifetime of that kind of fierce love wears you down. Even the strongest, most stubborn, willful adoration wilts. Overtime. It happens. The love is not lost it simply turns down the volume.
Nature and time see things differently. The well-oiled machine in sync with the needs of her child eventually breaks down. I can't compete with evolution.

I can't will it to stop, slow down. It does not listen. I cannot bear to lose the anchor, safe ground. I sob and sob until exhaustion sets in. I can't help myself.
Wrought with emotion. I overthink it. I think again, tricking the brain the inevitable won't happen. I can't even come close. In this life, I have loved many but only one burned constant. No matter, roles

were bartered away long ago. Overbearing, enveloping, tough, crazy mother love does not judge. It remains solid, no matter how deep the disappointment.

She watches quietly, observing the ebb and flow. Waiting patiently to gather the shattered, fallen pieces, dustbin in hand. What a sour burden to own something so precious, forced only to have to let it go. Her greatest gift, knowing precisely when to push and when to pull. That I understand. That, I know well. The incomparable fear of love and loss, one's heart ripped straight through the middle. Embers and ash. The unbearable, unbreakable mother-daughter bond, so simple and so complex.

don't call me daughter

I think it's safe to say I have an adequate grasp of the English language. I'm not a master or anything like that, but my vocabulary is mostly above average.

Words like resilient, thrive, and heal have recently got my head spinning, topsy-turvy.

I'm an unwilling survivor, scrappy I suppose. I get on with it most days, barrel my way through, above, over, break down the brick walls or slither under. Hey, whichever way is the quickest and least painful route.

Since as far back as memory allows and I can remember, I jump ahead. Literally, out of prickly sweet-smelling massive Evergreens, and figuratively, counting how many manipulative steps I need to hurry past the moment and get into the next.

The purple and vinyl a la Prince lusted raincoat I absolutely had to have during my teen angst dream years, or I would die on the spot. Literally, lie down, give up, quit, give in, be smothered, and forgotten. I got the coat, a Valentine's Day gift from a worried mom.

I didn't die right there, or then. Maybe I wore that coat five times, maybe less than that. Who's counting? It was a very long time ago, and a faded *if only* wish, the childlike impulsive desire and unhappy, happy memory.

It never *felt* comfortable that coat, it was stiff, the collar too high. The girls laughed and snickered like mean, insensitive kids do. I looked like a six-foot, odd shaped, out of place purple pill, or houseplant. The unsightly, spendthrift, unfashionable purchase quickly became another catastrophic loss of interest. The raincoat got tossed it in the attic closet, and discarded. I moved on and out.

It didn't *feel* satisfying, it didn't feel healthy or cool or resilient.

Nothing feels satisfying some thirty odd years later and many glorified, mystified, lusted objects and wants tossed aside. Every single thing happens *too late,* or *too early.* I've already moved on, and down the block.

Needless to say, I don't feel very resilient, or whole at the moment. That is precisely my problem. I'm not here, not really. My mind is never fully present. The wires are crossed, burnt, jumbled and fried. I am sick, they tell me. Or so they say. I'm not disagreeing so much; I hardly hear them anyway as my brain is already preoccupied with the million thoughts hitting me from every direction.

Sick? That is not okay, not allowed, and the foreign concept no matter how many times someone reminds me.

It's okay; it's not your fault. Really, how the hell would you know? Who the hell are you anyway?

I am not sure I am healthy or resilient enough.

Not inside my mind that moves faster than the fan spinning above at maximum velocity or the minutes, hours, ad nauseam days I want to hurtle over and straight through the sick parts.

"Don't patronize me," flies out of my mouth at the shrink's office before I can reel the words back in.

I knew they were coming; I'd already pre-calculated the scene, variables and walked through the scenario hours prior in my head. Yeah, I was way done before I walked through the door, and sat in the chair. I glanced at my mother, perhaps the only resilient, sturdy, good thing in my goddamn life and she knew. She understood I wasn't looking, wanting or needing an answer but a nod of reassurance.

My mother is elderly now, more tired and beaten down by life, cruel circumstance, hers and mine mixed together. She is the only one who sees the crazy, the horrific weight bearing ball and chain around my neck, the chills, terrors, paranoia and flights of fancy I have been. She knows. She understands. She sees who I am way before me. Without her strength I wonder, how do I carry on? Will I have the fortitude to care, to fight, to get on with it? To watch her crouched over the kitchen sink my head buried beneath a wet, cooling, soothing lavender washcloth is comforting and quieting.

I am unable to wallow in self-pity. I am less able to wallow, and more able to see what's in front of me. I am more and or less able.

There is no other you see, no other one, no person who grasps the chaotic concept that is me as well as she, as best as she or as devoted.

The Shape of Us

Watching my mother in the early evening hunched over the avocado, outdated sink grappling with her own physical limitations and pain preparing a salad, doing the dishes or whatever sense of comfort she finds in her daily routine, grants me serenity.

I find hope, resilience and strength in the sudsy water I have always known. Inside the familiar monotonous routine, I know I am loved and less alone. I am at peace in the quiet dusk hours of home.

I understand I will fight, the noise, the flashes of light and the bombardment bastard trickery of a broken mind not in isolation never alone, but with her by my side.

That coat, the one she bought ages ago when I was a spoiled teenage brat cost way too much. What I didn't know at the time was that she understood I was not just a spoiled rotten, self-absorbed teenage girl but that I wore my sadness on the inside.

Sadness I bore naked, unadorned, running fast and as far as I could to get away from myself. I didn't get very far at all, not really. The runner, running with scissors is a dangerous, treacherous path.

In the morning she looks my way smirking and shaking her head, "there's a rock in your bed." My mother still makes my bed. I can do it I know that, and so does she but she does it so much better. I let her for now because she can, it makes her feel good and because she's here a while longer.

I sleep with an oversize, jagged clouded Hunzite crystal under my pillow, and while my mom might think its silly fodder, she's grateful and relieved that I believe in something.

Any old thing, really. The vinyl, purple raincoat still hangs proudly in the attic because some old dreams should be kept and cherished until new ones take their place.

Even an eccentric, fleeting momentary lavender and pink rock can hold wisdom, resilience and healing wonder.

She made a divine pact that day, to lean into femininity and beauty and the body beautiful.

She would honor all her sisters faced with impossibly hard decisions.

The choice is solely and rightfully hers, and mine too.

Because only another woman truly understands the right to bear children, her body, her choice.

And only she gets to decide.

the inheritance tax

Please do not underestimate the fragile girl who has been broken.
The grown woman climbs barbed wire fences unapologetic, her jagged and cut limbs battle cries that honor the scars.
Bleeding profusely shrugging off the pain, she is awake and determined.
The girl is immune to the swirling, incessant noise hovering overhead.
Simply choosing to embrace the beautiful and worst kinds of misery.
Nah, man she's better than wasted breath.
Dancing the best soft shoe tap she can muster,
melody and movement sets her free.
Embers burn fast and hot as the dust piles grow mountains.
Molten ash reminders that blood dries to bone to dirt to swirling dust.
Just like that a solitary tree emerges from the sand and provides shelter.
The desert weeps evergreen, her inheritance tax.

"We are all disabled, broken parts, lost individuals, trying to find our way. Truth is what you know, here and happening now. There is only love and love is the bravest character of all."

—Georgia Pine

faded glory

There are a few things I know now by trial and error, when attention comes your way embrace it. Be brave enough to embrace and enjoy five minutes of some kind of fucked up fame, to be seen through the camera lens even while it steals a piece of your vulnerable heart and sacred soul. It's okay to try on different versions, experimenting behind platinum blond and a fuck you, this is me attitude.
Don't be ashamed or sad when the flash bulbs find a more interesting or louder subject. Be glad that you put yourself out there at all. But, know when it's time for introspection and more purposeful things, when your face/ body/ hair means little or next to nothing. Know when what you have to say means so much more. Know that when you're playing a part, the chameleon must shed its skin to begin again. Wait, and then release yourself from judgement and fear until you can sit comfortably alone. Safe and happy inside a body that is strong and healthy, and a heart that seeks kindness instead of accolades. It might take a long, long, long while to really find the woman you're looking for. She's out there, no longer hiding, or locked in. Don't wait twenty years or fifty, or eighty more, to be OK with the unique body, hair and face that you are. Don't starve yourself, or hide inside oversized sweats. Don't worry about the next it girl, because her day passes too. Time does not stay stuck; we must change and grow to get unstuck. We're shape-shifters passing through, images fading, forgotten photographs. The sparkles of human dust kindness you leave for a young girl to discover in the dirt are the bursts of sunshine and sparkling black diamond dust wisdom. Falling through tiny fingers as wonder and Deja vu forms a knowing smile on tender lips. They know intrinsically, soulfully and mindfully that you were here. Don't ask me how, they just do.

little black dress

Sexy lives under an elegant black dress and self-confidence.

Sexy is alive inside the mystery of courting and discovery.

Sexy does not need to be tits and ass on full display.

Call me old-fashioned, that's fine.

I am.

A romantic moment should be shared exclusively between you and him.

The undressing, tremors of excitement and passion remain an intimate dance.

Don't try to dress up or down, and never sell yourself short to please him.

Do not throw away your most intimate parts.

You will need them.

You'll grow old someday, like me.

Your skin will most certainly sag, you'll get cellulite, wrinkles and belly rolls.

But no one, absolutely no one owns the right to your body.

It is the precious, perfect, loving and loyal home for your soul.

the highway halfway mark

I wonder, I do. I cannot help but wonder what's down the road from the place I have ever truly called home. The wood and grass and nails and bolts, the wet familiar dew smells and giggling baby sounds. The joy and the sorrow. I can't help but observe and wonder. The funny, peculiar, crooked way of seeing the world that is all my own. The structure has cracks, fissures, and deep gaping holes, pockets that need love and attention, there are patching and mending to be done. I don't know if I have enough glue stored in the chicken coop to hold the facade together before the walls come crumbling down. I am for better or worse, at the highway halfway mark.
I mind I do, at times. I mind a lot.
Sometimes, I don't mind at all. I laugh and live, and get lost in the hilarious, fleeting moments. I get scared, frightened, and paralyzed too. Funny, I was never scared as a child. I was wild, fearless, fierce, and strong.
Maybe I greedily used up all the miles and worn down the treads on my running shoes. New Balance 574's. There's nowhere, no road, no mountain, no distances left, no place far and enough away to hide.
That's okay. It's all right. I do get tired sometimes. Mostly, I wish I could bottle up the Lupita lovely creature cuddled beside me. Her warmth and heat and breath and beating heart radiate and rejuvenate my childlike spirit. Her smile makes me weepy. I can't. I can't keep her here with me.
I cannot understand the death concept, wrap my head around this curious mystery called life. I try, but maybe I can't comprehend a life without all the people and places I have cherished and loved. Close, always close by even when separated by continents and telephone lines.

Jacqueline Cioffa

My mother and I don't see eye to eye on so many things. I talk too much, worry too much, cry too much, am crazy too much and yet she is here in her first forever home and mine folding the laundry. Her pace slow, her gait sad, her grit defeated and still she is cemented together, red brick stronger than I. She realizes her halfway mark has long expired, and that makes me hold my breath.

As if I could stop time between the inhale and exhale before the next.

As if. I'm stalling, still. Silly me, I am a grownup woman who's not very grownup at all. I understand that hanging on tight to the breath is wishful thinking and I will most surely pass out. I can't help be hopeful and delusional at times. It hurts to catch my breath.

Here, at the highway halfway mark.

vainglorious

A sister recently said to me, "you're vain." I was shocked.

I never, ever thought of myself that way.

I mulled it over in my head, and guess what?

I am vain.

Women need to be vain. When I was young, I should've been proud and more confident with my skinny body and face instead of constantly apologizing for the way I looked. Just the other day, a woman made a snide comment when I joked about 'getting older and fat.' Fat was a poor choice of words; I work hard in the gym and always have. I eat healthy, don't drink, and don't smoke. I live clean and quiet.

So, fuck-off for my slenderness, my beauty, my femininity. I'm done apologizing. And to my twenty-year-old self, I'm so sorry I didn't appreciate your privileged supermodel self. I wish I'd been happier, less judgy, and grateful with the woman in the mirror. The one I was *forever* trying to keep up with, a fantastical, unrealistic image I suppose.

Today, I'm shooting for vainglorious. No longer apologizing for taking care of my fifty-year-old self, far from the critics, naysayers and judgement. I am leaning in, and no longer covering up all the curves and soft sides.

beautiful you

There is a lack of elegance, sexiness and mystery missing in photographs of women today, especially celebrities and the overexposed, blasé way they brand themselves and how they are portrayed through the lens.
Social media and fashion have made women seem like untouchable objects, loud, fake and even desperate at times.
The "look at me" culture screaming for more and more attention.
I have always had a more hate than love relationship with modeling and fame.
Yes, I realize that sounds trite.
I was a model, white and privileged.
But I was a young, impressionable girl, who today is a woman with decades away from the spotlight by choice and a fresh perspective.
I wonder when future generations look back at images of women will they be curious, or exhausted by the sheer volume?
I can only appreciate now the mystique of a three am shoot in Milan, a lost era and the simple gesture of adjusting a dress, caught and frozen in time by the keen eye of a sharp photographer.
Women are magical creatures, real and raw and the most beautiful when unaware of themselves.
They do not need a movement to define their power; they have been beautiful, raw, strong, passionate warriors for centuries and centuries birthing ideals, children, and nurturing souls.
Less is more, so do not ever undervalue or compare yourself to someone else's million followers.
Find your own unique way, and remember true beauty is forevermore.

girl in progress

May we be your best example of speaking the ugly truth
May you never be soiled or spoilt or talked into anything tawdry
May you remain untainted and uninhibited in all your glorious nakedness
Never know shame by the hands or wants or manipulation of another fucker
Man, oh man
May you never hear great tits and ass when you walk down the street
in your skinny jeans and heels
May you always find the courage to say NO
I'm out of here
Punk ass douchebag
I own my identity
May your virgin innocence remain crystalline pure
And unshaken and untouched and untaken
Until YOU decide
Owning your sexuality
May the warriors and feminists
who spoke out before you
with their brokenness and battle scars
Screaming no way, fuck off, not me
I'm out of here
Daughters
You are the white warriors, the reason and hope
Not this time, never again, no dirty little secrets
You remain forever sacred and pure

luck be a lady

Authenticity.

I've been thinking a lot lately about the word, gargling, swishing it around in my mouth and spitting it out.

If I only show you the photoshopped, concealed, makeup pretty me you'll never understand the underbelly. The crunchy grit, rawness hidden beneath. The really good stuff, the honest kind that matters. Most days I can only see how my illness defines me. Every single piece that's been stolen, the immeasurable, inexplicable loss of self. The shame, self-hatred, feelings of worthlessness, doubt, insecurities, paranoia, fear, inappropriate remarks, irrational behavior and the myriad of negatives that live inside my broken, chaotic mind. Not to mention the physical excruciating pain, dizziness, anxiety, numbness, sweats, chills. Or the *forty-ish* pounds of added weight, the personal incessant reminder of the unworthy scales. When matters of life and death happen, I stopped counting pounds. I admit it, I cry, hide my face in shame, live with resentment and assumed the worst. I'm a girl, it must be my fault.

That's not what *this* day or this piece is about. Today is about threading the needle and the incredible luck I've been dealt. Yes, *luck*. *Lucky to be born a lady with free will who's figuring it out.*

stomping ground

The first closed fist came fast and without warning.
The one-two successions of hate and rage pummeling my face. Fast, too fast, so sudden, bruising my ribs and squashing self-love and confidence dwelling inside my envious, almost six-foot frame.
Blood dribbled down my chin, I was out of my mind with fear; I lay paralyzed as a friend pried off this ugly stranger.
The door slammed.
Silence.
Shhh, be quiet do not make a sound.
I could not move, I was paralyzed, shell-shocked and alone.
Alone, all alone in a foreign land that was not my home. I was far, far, far from the limitless love of my father's face and the tenacious, fierce protection of my mother's love.
I wanted them.
At that moment, I wanted nothing more.
I was trapped inside a dungeon with steel bars wrapped around my brain, stuck in self-hate and fear.
I could not find one crack in the dark thinking, one sliver of me.
I was nineteen years old. I was skinny. I was statuesque. I was stunning. I was a model. I was the stuff of a supermodel. I was liquid gold.
I had everything I ever wanted in front of me.
Or so I was told.
The model with the eggplant, swollen eye and collagen plump perfect split lip got exactly what she deserved. She must have.
Right?
Isn't that what they say, wasn't she the cliché?
She started referring to herself in the third person.
She'd forgive him. She'd stay, too terrified to run.

She was movement while motionless. She was stuck in a cage with menacing black crows, words like duty, responsibility, and blame circling overhead.
The feisty, funny, freckle-faced girl was gone. The one who dreamt in color falling in love with art and music, and all the wrong men. She thought they might see her, really see her, you know, past the face to her insides. She wanted to feel like the low notes of the most haunting and bittersweet melody that made her weep.
She wanted to weep for all the right reasons, be moved by a love song.
Her pitiful attempts to feel something like healthy love were sugar cravings, and she was allergic to white, empty carbs.
The blows softened over time and became fatal, venom verbal daggers.
She preferred the punch; at least she felt less numb, less than nothing.
The bruises had been visible on her invisible, disappearing skin. Her shoulders curled in self-protection, she pretended they were white angel wings keeping her safe while she gazed down at the sidewalk or out or anywhere but inward, avoiding all eye contact. Who was this person? She doesn't recognize her at all.
Oh yeah, The Master of Pretending.
To live, to exist in the dark requires discipline.
The first time someone stomped on her innocence, she barely remembers. When you're a child figuring stuff out, boundaries and boundaries are muddy waters. She had placed her whole intact self, the beauty, purity, and bliss in someone else's hands.
Isn't that the most natural thing a child can do?
The girl with the spitfire imagination who ate cartwheels and giggles for breakfast wasn't born into a world filled with hate, fear, skepticism and all the negatives.
No, those feelings were learned.
She left the atrocious man-boy crusher of spirits, eventually.
It took time, a long, long while for the metal bars to rust, and to feel her heart smile properly for the first time.
To choose the slightest possibility of a different way of thinking. She's not so perfect anymore, but to me, she's prettier than before. She picks up the pre-fight, pre-conditioning, worn, torn leather

boxing gloves and sets them aside, cautiously, by her dressing table filled with different weapons of choice.
Amethyst stones, prisms, healing crystals, gems, pink quartz healing,
Zen rocks, Buddhas, and a picture frame she glances at each night.
Wrapped in her daddy's protective, safe arms is a gleeful little girl whispering, "you are all that's innocent, good and kind.
You are here, remember, you are worthy. You are loved.
You deserve a hug."
That girl?
She's all mine.

I'm a humanist who happens to be a GIRL.

This body of mine carried me through days of sophisticated lies and ambition. This body of mine has been home to shame, trials and tribulations. This body of mine has known love and felt all woman. But, this body of mine cannot and does not coexist without the messy, chaotic, beautiful, strong-minded masculine pushing forward and walking her through a new, more experienced chapter. Onward, in these bizarre times, and an overtly strange millennium.

yes mother

Behind every mother, there is despair and strength.
Behind every mother, there are tears of joy and pride.
Behind every mother, trash bins wait to be emptied, mountains of dirty laundry to be washed, and meals cooked.
It is a dirty, thankless job being a yes mother.
Twenty-four hours is not enough time to cleanse, renew, and release the dirty business of mothering.
To properly moisturize and ready oneself for the day.
I am the daughterless child with time to give away.
Lean on me, I don't care if I have to get my manicured hands dirty.
I will give you some of my abundant hours.
I will take out the trash, and do the menial tasks to free up part of your day.
To breathe in responsibility.
The dark hours can wait.
Tomorrow will come, and she starts all over again.
The yes mothers, the matriarchs, the collectors of trash and menders of bloody knees.
The seamstresses of broken hearts.
The yes mothers' live lives of faith and purpose, with little reward.
Being a mother is not the prettiest thing about her.
Being a yes mother, being a matriarch is the prettiest thing about her even when it's hard.
A mother's ability to forever reach towards the sun, in spite of forgotten dreams and tragic fate.
She does not dwell on mistakes in her house and tosses regret in the trash every day.
One single, plastic bag problem at a time.
Just the one, day after monotonous day.

Sorrow may visit her home, but it cannot stay.
She will not have it.
Shadow love says we're all different, but a yes mother's love says we're all the same.
Matriarchs, even on the bad days.

against the current

There comes a point in life when you must accept the reality and the gift that is the passage of time.
While I know in my heart, our time grows shorter and shorter I can't help but be bitchy, mean, selfish and lose my patience daily. I have not been the easiest child.
The woman who birthed me has been a mother since she could walk, and always has my back even as hers continues to shrink in size but never stature.
If you're lucky enough to grow up as you grow old, there are many vital lessons to be earned.
Humility, integrity, kindness, strength, how to find the micro-moments of joy, and how to let go of the pain and anxiety for a little while.
I am not a mother, but I understand better now the role of matriarch. And it's a doozy.
Life is hard, brutal and no one escapes tragedy.
Some of us learn to carry it better, stronger and with a healthy dose of humor.
I'm not that strong, or that good but I hope a little bit of her backbone remains fused to mine.
We are after all strong swimmers, and she taught me how to stay afloat.

the shadow of her grace

To the most beautiful girl with the gypsy mane and wild heart
Sister of my soul
When I'm having a bad day, I will think of you
With so much love, grit, and admiration
Too young to go, too young to die, too young to miss all the magic you gave so freely
Your sweetness, strength and absolute authenticity made us better
You are so much better than most
Noble and kind
Cancer does not win
Even though you are transitioning
You win
You do
Fuck cancer
You get to keep all the joy and the curiosity and sunshine you shared
So Sweetly
My heart breaks knowing you won't
Be here now
That your pretty face won't pop up while scrolling my screen
Knowing we walked the earth at the same time makes my heart happy
Swollen with emotion
And a little bit somber and teary for your family and friends
Especially your mama
I send her all my strength and this prayer of gratitude
A mother shouldn't have to say goodbye first
I wish her all my strength and energy
I will try to stay present and mindful

on the hard days
Aware of life's challenges and gifts
I will look for you in the simple moments
In the changing leaves, spring blossoms, and wild Mustangs
I will remember you, always
Pole dancing and smiling and soaring
Shining organic and authentic
Go ahead and let go
You're not leaving just transitioning
The air will taste sweeter on the other side
The ocean and sun will shine transcendent, the brightest colors of turquoise and gold
All the love you gave so generously remains
I promise to seek out your light in all the crevices and cracks where fear and darkness try to grow
Warriors never surrender forever seeking higher ground
Majestic and proud
I carry your spirit inside the joy and temporary little things
I am better for knowing you
I am better for knowing you walked this earth so graciously
We are all better because you were brave enough to share your journey
Your heroic fight
The good, the horrific, and the mystical moments
So I say goodbye for now
It was an honor to walk the same earth
With only the most sincere gratitude and love
I am grateful for the blessings and life lessons shared
Walking beside you in awe of your strength, and beauty
In the shadow of your grace

I am learning to let go of who and what no longer fits, and suddenly like magic I'm surrounded by good, caring people.

I am, I am learning.

She disappeared inside the land of make-believe, filled with Crayola crayons so bright she wore tinted sunglasses

Nope. Not this time.

corsets and candy

I would like to lead a dark, sophisticated life
I dream of a fancy lady in spiked heels, red nails and lips and such
She wears corsets to breakfast
and dines on champagne and caviar
I run away from fame and all its trappings
I'm a messy sneaker-wearing practical jeans girl
transparent to the touch
I don't need a prince charming just a sweet whisper
A subtle nod, bittersweet embrace
Ask me to cross an ocean and I'd do it for you
Even for just five minutes
I don't care I'm not proud though I am scared
I'm sophisticated just enough

you're a knockout

I could tell you all the things I despise about my body, all the ways I've mistreated it. I could tell you how much I have hated it, and still do. This isn't that story. The insecure girl who never felt skinny enough, pretty enough, or comfortable in her skin. Time passes fast, and I wish I could tell that awkward girl all the beautiful, precious things I know only now about her body. How it would keep her healthy, and strong. How her legs wouldn't buckle when death, loss, and despair found her. How her flabby arms no longer crossed tightly in self-protection, but open wide. I would tell her to keep her chin up, her shoulders back, and her back straight. She would need all her strength, limbs and muscles to navigate this crazy life. Keep her feet rooted firmly to the ground, and arms raised triumphantly. This body is her home, however temporary, housing her soul, and the gatekeeper to her radiant beauty. Her spirit shines and her body breathes life through its veins, muscles, blood, and heart, even when she is holding her breath. I would tell her not to be so hard on herself, and that I love her any old way.

"Make peace with all the colors of you, even the indigos, greys and threatening black hues"

mother, may i

Your love is tearing me apart. Wide open flood gushes of white, transparent bubble love overflowing magnificent from beyond the ethers. I didn't know, I couldn't understand how gut wrenching, excruciating it was for you to say good-bye.

I wasn't even a concept.

You knew me, already. I was in your best laid plans, secret, subconscious desires. I was your home, your perfect glass house vision where fishhooks and dinner bell chimes rang happy.

I'm so very sorry; my heart is split open wide. I didn't understand the pain you felt when you closed your forever eyes. To slumber, but not leave to sleep, to miss the moments, and the chance to kiss and hug your life goodnight.

I couldn't; I didn't know about you. The beautiful, erect, stately presence that would shine blinding, the rough diamond reminder, illuminating the same walls and floors I would walk upon. The grass you planted lovingly, the roses you cured and cultivated. The manhattans you enjoyed, and sweet-smelling molasses legacy. The tender smell of lilac breeze, so calming and familiar when I close my eyes.

I'm sorry. I'm so sorry I didn't see me inside your eyes. How could I?

Jacqueline Cioffa

I guessed you might be near; goose bump clues and suspicions. The ever-curious offspring, questioning the elegant, graceful ways you walked through a simple, stately life.

I was too busy running and monopolizing time. Tick tock, clock. Time to say hello, and goodbye.

I'm not a child, anymore. Am I?

I'm sorry I wasn't there to understand the pain of saying goodbye too soon, your babies they'd miss out on all the delightful days and days stripped, gut ripped of your presence.

I'm sorry I didn't understand *your* pain, your tears, your grief, and your life.

Until now, I am seeing you living for the first time.

And understanding. My open heart is bursting. The tears flooding, I cry, are yours, not mine.

I couldn't know the unbreakable, nylon thread that forever connects us; would be the very best part of you, and the holiest, treasured, most sacred part of me.

I couldn't know the unbearable, gut-wrenching mother-daughter bond. The heartbreaking pure pretty, precious perfect, lofty weight we would share divided from opposite understanding, and heaven's ends.

I have loved you more than I can bear, without question.

Mother, may I call you mother even if you never belonged to me, only indirectly?

The Shape of Us

You belonged to her, and she is the most exquisite gift you could have given. From here, and somewhere beyond orbital rotations, ever changing seasons and square boxes. Where glass houses are only silly, fanciful dream figments of an overactive, exuberant, well-meaning child's imagination.

I will find you, and her, again, in the ethers. I will run to you from the other side, arms open and beaming. I never understood until the floodgates broke open, and I felt your love encompassing me inside the bubble, protective, loving and quieting.

Your life cut short, sweet regret rushing through my blood and veins, into my pulsating, welcoming, pumping heart alive. I feel you, and the walls come crashing down.

I won't forget. I won't. I won't forget one, single memory from her to you. The glass house belongs to the present inhabitants, and the stars shine lovely and transparent here from my side.

I won't give up. I won't waste my time. I will embrace the thorn, prickly pain and the mind blinding joy. I promise.

Divinely, sublimely and with the grace of a God you whisper in my dreams, feminine divine.

sky's no limit

No matter who you are or where you come from, you're bound to be judged.

That's the ugly business of being a strong woman with dreams, desires, visions, ideas, opinions and a voice.

Remember you are fierce, powerful and worthy.

Never apologize for breaking the glass, the sky is your limitless ceiling.

toxic lady

Kindness and self-confidence become the noose around my neck in a shallow world filled with self-absorbed, self-obsessed, fear-fueled desperate "look at me" cries for attention
Girl guilty
I try not to dwell on the fake realities,
about you or her in their filtered out of focus world, as redundant images scroll past my screen
An overwhelming, weight-bearing, heart heavy sadness floods my brain connecting bones and boiling blood
Social media may very well be the death of me
Isolation, extreme isolation hides behind the famous faces of one million followers and me
It is the most toxic thing about me
I take breaks so I can breathe, searching out the sun and trees and oxygen
And some goddamn authenticity
I do not give two fucks about some billion-dollar makeup queen, Yeezys, Cannes, or Louboutin's
I do not care one bit about the latest fashion fad or how much money you make or the fabulous party people you call 'framily'
High school was a lifetime ago, time to grow up and put on big girl panties
It's too much fake news when one is searching for a higher purpose
We're all dying the same shit and piss unavoidable last breath
The more time I live in stillness and honor the grass under my feet
The more I understand kindness, honor, beauty, love, and acceptance cannot be felt through a computer screen
Walking and talking feels better when looking up
Not down

I wonder what they will think of me and my digital footprint in a hundred years
Absolutely nada, zilch, nothing
There is freedom and wisdom and acceptance in that
I hope that I can grow old gracefully, without the want or need of someone else's perception of my femininity
We can never really know which lies or truths exist inside somebody else's story
Living simple stripped down and exposed
Is the most beautiful validation and transitory truth
I can be
Outed from behind a computer screen

sister of my soul

Excuse me, do I know you?
I vaguely remember your face
We were friends once, the very best friends
We were tight, so very close
Secrets were shared, tears cried, belly laughs burned and drunken nights felt never-ending
Even faded rock star blue jeans with holes in the knees passed back and forth between us
Shared like too many frozen margaritas
And raucous giggles on easy, breezy sunny Friday summer afternoons
Until you were gone, an empty barstool
Poof
Snuffed out like the American Spirit we'd split
I hated you
I fucking hated you with every fiber of my being
Resentment, anger, jealousy filled my gut
Making me ugly
The dark circles under my eyes blackened and grew angrier than a looming stormy night
I despised you for giving up
Weren't the decades spent together a la Sex and the City worthy of a text, an email, or a quick two-second voicemail?
Was I worth less than a penny of your precious, busy time?
Copper erodes and turns green acrid
Like the brain matter moving too fast in head and scrabbling my mind
I hurled paranoia and accusations into the air as the mania swept me away

The Shape of Us

Wiping out any semblance of the me I once was
The me I once was
I'm still me I screamed
I'm right here
The same me
The one you were so comfortable with even sharing the same cowboy boots
Oh how I fucking hated your guts for years and years
The hate festered into blame and disgust
I despised myself, deemed unworthy
Crying myself to sleep lost in the disease I didn't ask for
Moving, crawling, retreating under the bed sheets
Into a cocoon of safety
Home
Back to small town living where blaring sirens, whirring taxis and loud, overcrowded subways no longer made me dizzy
The nauseating velocity no longer unmanageable
Sadness crept out of my bones taking up residence for good
Rapid cycling and insomnia became my new BFF companions
Still, I hated your fucking selfish, ugly, uncompassionate guts
Every single one of you, every cheesy Intsagram photo with the old posse made me sick
How were you all happy?
Moving on without me, together, living, loving, smiling
How could you?
Was it that easy, or was it that necessary?
Was I the inconvenience, the nuisance?
Was I better forgotten
Sisters of my soul went missing
A slap, I still feel the sting
I longed for mended relationships, shared lipsticks, Mani Pedi dates, girl talk
Vacations to exotic beaches, Mexican beer and tacos, lazy beach afternoons
I still miss it
I can't help it
I still get weepy and blue
I didn't get it

Jacqueline Cioffa

I couldn't understand
It was I who went missing
Not you and you and you
I had to drop the hate into a bucket of fish guts hurling it out to sea
with my sins,
sickness, resentment and harsh judgment
To see sunny, aqua blue
Sisters of my soul
The ones that count
Are still here
Rooting me on, a phone call away
They never gave up experiencing all the colors I wear
At lightning speed
And annoyingly snail slow
They don't mind when I speak too fast, or cry too long
They don't care when I forget little things
When my damaged mind can't quite keep up
They see my soul shine, both pretty and disastrous
They love me anyway, no matter how busy or distracted
Maybe I asked too much forgotten sisters of my soul
Or maybe I hated myself a little too much
Resentment, jealously and anger festered inside far too long
I am growing too weary and too old to hold tight to the past
Sisters come and go
Some sisters came and went before I got the chance to say goodbye
and hello
I don't regret one minute in their company
My soul shines the same
Sickly or healthy
I am perfectly, imperfect and that is my right
My authentic beauty
Life is hard, mystical, magical, beautiful, trying and tragic
Be here now
I must
Be here now
As it should be
Be here now
Because being here right now cuts the ties that bind and burn

The Shape of Us

Finding my tribe
The ones that love me
For the way I glow is light and lovely reciprocated
Sisters of my soul
To the beauties who came before
I thank you
For clearing a path
And opening a window to a different road
My soul has more room to grow and share
So long, old familiar sisters travelling parallel roads
Separate, and independent
I smile releasing the memories
Just like that hate and jealousy dissipate into a cloud of white fog
freedom
I am home, whole
On the inside

Jacqueline Cioffa

in between the rain

Have I been good enough, Mother?
Oh how I miss the days when your skin was smooth, and bronzed
How your smile beamed when you saw my little face
Remember when you let me stay up late, way, way past bedtime
To watch scary movies curled up on the cozy couch, giggling in horror
Eating popcorn and pretend hiding under the covers
Safe and secure in your strong embrace
Oh, how I miss the days when I had to crook my neck way up to look at your face
Today, I tower and hover above your small, fragile frame
Have I been good enough, Mother?
When you let me play outside with the boys, and beat them at their stupid, army games
You taught me strength, and how not to be scared
You gave me courage in spades
Fearless, I was
I wonder were you ever afraid?
Placing my spoilt wants, silly desires and pipe dreams ahead of yours
Have I been good enough, Mother?
That I deserved my beautiful, eloquent God-given birth name
When I ached to run off, to take off and discover life
At too early an age to understand big words like prolific and egotistic
To comprehend what the world meant, what strangers were all about?
To carve out a space, a place, a home of my very own
Independent from the safety net of family barbecues, water pistol

The Shape of Us

fights, and summertime rainbow sprinkles
To jump willingly under the sprinklers
My face was soft and sweet back then
Innocent and kind
In between the rain
Have I been good enough, Mother?
The strangers I would meet never calling me by my birth name
Only you
And your stoic hidden pain, discomfort, fear, pride and worry
Would use my birthright, proper name
In times of distress, joy or exasperation
Yes, I know
I understand
I exasperated your patience with my stubbornness
I could be cruel, selfish at times, my face no longer childlike
I had grown cold
In between the rain
The puddles became too deeply complicated to navigate
I fell short too many times
Soaking my sobbing, acrid broken heart
In disillusionment and despair
I loved you then, Mother
When I screamed and howled your name
The miles and miles separating us
Growing continents and dust storms evermore
Distant, though never apart
Have I been good enough, Mother?
When I married the wrong man who beat me down
Leaving bitterness, and resentment underfoot
Still, you watched and waited
Strong and steady for the both
Patient enough, praying enough and hoping enough
I would find my own way
Time would not be kind
To you, to me, to us
Yet there would always be a steady, solemn love and quiet grace
Forevermore
Blinding beauty on the sunny days and even under the downpours

Disease would creep in, stealing my father's good nature
And saddening your face with age
The lines etching and crevicing deep
In between the rain
The mistakes of a lifetime read like tea leaves on your wistful cheeks
While my skin remained smooth, not yet fully broken
Have I been good enough, Mother?
When you sat beside my bedside and watched
As your precious, precocious
Daughter went insane
Drowning in trenches and invisible caverns of madness
Remembering less and less her own name
Her identity, stolen but not forgotten
Intertwined and familiar by the markings on your
Stunning, freckled face
Still waters and gyre currents cannot steal away true beauty
I see you buried beneath the layers and layers of family
Replaced now with a hurry-cane
And a frail, hunched over, less able gait
That makes me cringe with fear
The time passage closing
In between the rain
I will try to be patient, more patient
Then I have been
I will try hard, harder
Have I been good enough, Mother?
Kind enough?
Sincere enough?
Polite enough?
Rolling my eyes in frustration by your deafened ears
Repeated sentences, and failing eyesight
As closed captions scroll across the screen
Oh fuck, I have not
I have not
Been
Good enough
I have been
Selfish

The Shape of Us

Losing myself somewhere
In between the rain
The seasons came too fast, too furious, and too mean
Upon us
To be anything but
Your child
You, the giver of birth
The bearer of the light and dark that dances
Upon my soul
Inside your little girl's heart lives joy and sorrow
She is all grown up
Almost
Always looking forwards and back
Asking one simple question
Have I been good enough, Mother?
Have I been half as good as you?
Have you lived a purposeful life, filled with love and admiration?
A life worth living
In between the rain
The seasons will bury us
I love my birth name, truly I do
The life you gave so freely
I will carry
In between the mudslides, the dew, the frost,
And the singularly, unique snowflakes
As we wait for the sun
The speckled sunbeams you so adore
I learned golden admiration from you
Have I been good enough, Mother?
I will not abandon you
Not now, not tomorrow
Not when it would be so easy
To walk away
Not when it counts
We're made from the same together, tougher stock
In between the rain
You mother, have been so much more than good
Enough

Jacqueline Cioffa

You have been
My one and only regret
To not find you
In between the rain
When the seasons change
As the minutes tick-tock, deafening in my ear
I cannot stop the stupid clock
For, if I could
I would be good enough, Mother
To halt the rise and fall of time
To be happy inside and out
In between the rain and her teardrops

my first bff, and forever friend

If I could give you one thing
And only one
It would be the eyes of your mother
Beaming with pride
At the glamorous, vulnerable, capable, solid, loyal, stylish, kind and beautiful daughter you are
To watch you grow up so pretty
Comfortable in your very own skin
To see you paint the world with all the bright and shining colors you've collected and earned
Has been a fantastical honor
Even while navigating your way through the dark
Without losing your bursting heart
If I could show you how truly beautiful you are in your granny nightgown laughing out loud, watching tv, barefaced and carefree
My dearest, cherished and forever friend
I would gladly buy you fifty mirrors
One for every year
Every milestone, every memory
You are your mother's one and only
Her grandest treasure
And so tonight, I summon all the angels to send her your way
Waking you with a kiss while you sleep
On this, the eve of your birth
I love you now, and forever
Until you meet her again

The she devil lives on me. Even on a good day I cannot shake her. I wouldn't want to.

stay wild and free

my body, my choice

Dear God,

I haven't been talking to you much.
I'm sorry I haven't been in touch.
I lost my faith for a long while.
I lost myself, too.
I forgot I was your perfect creation.
I forgot the privilege it is to be female.
I forgot I was able to create life, to make another human.
Wow, what a miracle and awesome gift you gave this body of mine.
I did not love her with all my power and weight and conviction.
I did not honor her the way she deserved.
Her beauty was lost under the pummeling fists of an angry man.
An ugly man who would break her lip, her spirit, and her desire to celebrate all things feminine.
She would learn to cower, to hide and to hate all men, abused and terrified.
Years would pass, while her self- loathing, and self-worth only intensified.
Defeated, she still slept in his bed, crying herself to sleep after every violation.
Why, God, why me?
Asks another girl in another town, in some other awful, God-forsaken grotesque situation.
She was late.
Oh dear God, no, no, no.
Her period did not come.
She prayed and begged mercy.

Unsure she could carry this child born of hate, from a monster.
She was conflicted and terrified.
She prayed on her knees, begging and bartering.
She made a promise.
She and I, we promised together and our strength amplified.
God, if you make me bleed, I will leave this vicious cycle of damnation.
She woke, undies stained red and smiled through tears for the first time.
There would be no more rape, no more abuse, no more night terrors.
She was lucky and packed her bags good riddance.
We made a divine pact that day, to lean into femininity, and beauty and the body beautiful.
She would honor all her sisters faced with hard choices.
They were solely her choices, and solely mine, not his to carry.
Because only another woman truly understands the right to bear children, or not.
And only she gets to decide.

Can you believe someone once said to me, ***"You're skinny, you don't have any problems?"***

...as if being a lunatic and a woman wasn't hard enough

dance party

Make sure when you play dress up, make your face pretty, and paint your eyes the colors of your soul you recognize the true, unique beauty behind the smoke and mirrors.
Embrace the big belly laughs, slip-ups, insecurities, and vulnerable girly silliness...
Rise and lift your head towards the sun... true beauty lives inside the recesses of fine lines, heartfelt tears, risks taken, lived and embraced straight from the heart.
Find the joy, pull your shoulders back, stand tall and let yourself bask in the light, beautiful girl. Loving the whole package takes a whole lot of time, strength and bon-vivant-courage.
Go on, get it, girl.
Treat yourself to the finest riches, luxurious and spoiled indulgences. Throw a face-painting, dance-it-out, dress-me-up, big girl party.
One that screams...
Look, mom, "I'm all grown up!"

"I want to live simple. I want orange and red leaves and high school football and small-town life. I want to erase the days lived in the hollow and free my mind and body from the trickery of a fast life. I am throwing out the Gucci shoes and Prada bags and the heavy burden and the in crowd."
    —The Red Bench: A Descent And Ascent Into Madness

if the shoe fits

I couldn't help but notice the pretty, cool chick in line at the grocery store in front of me and her platform, wooden clogs. Maybe she's from NYC, definitely not from around here, (most sensible people wear Timberlands). The streets are a sheet of ice. She's going to fall on her ass outside. I had just fallen on mine.
A disabled man was having trouble paying and checking out. The cool chick was there in two seconds flat, "I've got this. Let me pay for this."
Well, well, hello sister. The man could not have been happier…she made his day, the cashiers and mine. If the shoe fits, wear it loud and proud.

Jacqueline Cioffa

bad bitches

Wouldn't it be lovely if kindness, loyalty, and showers of affection were the norm and everyday reality?
Wouldn't it be cool to be female without an edge?
Wouldn't it be awfully nice to let your guard down?
Security lives in the company of my shadow.
My twenty-pound puppy, smiling, wag tailing, tongue licking, furball companion.
Lupita lovely teaches me patience, confidence, and authenticity.
A refreshing kind of love that is pure and uncomplicated.
For one glorious moment I forget, all the exhausting, ugly, insecure woman parts.
With her, I'm free to be me.
On the walk.
In sweats, no makeup and sneaks, I'm relaxed and at ease.
I don't care how I look on the outside, and neither does she.

gum on your shoe

If you can live with gum on your shoe, sweat on your brow and frown lines quivering from your lip, well then, I can too.
You are a cautionary tale of the worst and best kind of chaos, tortured buried secrets and lies.
Brush off the shit and the stink, unmasking your truth.
Embrace the planetary spins and celebrate silver linings.
Be better than me, bigger, and more evolved.
Be good. Be kind. Be cool. Be true.
By being you.
I'll walk beside you, shitstorms and all.
Freestyling, freethinking and freewheeling.
This is our time around.

Jacqueline Cioffa

beauty reigns optimistic

Forgive me if I cannot turn a blind eye.
In time I will most assuredly be ready to leave this existence light-years behind.
An old woman whose lens has grown blurry and irises cry, whose ears ring incessant, suffering too many sounds of despair.
She dreams of a place far better than here where gardenia blossoms in winter, stardust colors her veins electric and children play without fear.
There are no guns, diversity, or hatred and money is a forgotten concept.
Beauty reigns optimistic.

hello, dolly

You are not your pain
It is not the total of all the beautiful that is you
When burdens become hard to carry
Like some days do
Open your arms and unclench your fists
Bury the heavy in the dirt beside mine
So that you might remember
Joy lives here too
Go ahead close your eyes
Rewind to a time when you smiled
In spite of yourself
Back to a day when you laughed for the hell of it
Sweet and smooth surrender
Releasing the maudlin blues
It's hard to choose happiness when you think you don't deserve it
But you do
Life is heavy girl
So why not lighten up
It's okay to be a little sad
When you leave room for a little happy too

Jacqueline Cioffa

my girl gone missing

Oh dear how I miss you
My precious girl gone missing
Back home inside the spirit realm
Where they wait patiently for an A+ okay sign
from me
That I am strong enough to go it alone
To do life on my own
Bittersweet goodbyes from beyond
That is on me
To sever interstellar ties that bind
To think how selfish I was all this time holding on so tight
To your death, DNA and cellular memory
All the while your loud love tap on my shoulder
The playful and annoying living and breathing reminder
That
I am not dead
Just yet
But
That you are
Heed the ghostly whispers whistling on the wind
Hush now
It's perfectly fine to hang onto the memories
But it's high time to let go
You human are doing just fine on your own
Besides
There are 777 lifetimes between us
Sometimes separate and others bound too tight together
Making it hard to distinguish where one life ends and another
begins

The Shape of Us

Never forget
I have loved you
I have loved you so
I have been loved so well, my ghosts
For that I thank you
Cherishing our time together in the here and now
Go ahead and move on
I understand
I am alive without you
Beyond the ether, I cannot go

radical acceptance

I hope the world she lives in is a kinder place to dwell. I pray the blue people have learned compassion towards the disabled, the weak, and the mind sick. I hope that time has made her world a softer, more humane place to visit. Where race, judgment, shame, and fear have been obliterated from her planet, coloring her life with only jovial minutes. She will grow up to be a robust woman, a great healer, fearless traveler, headstrong warrior and the gypsy traveling the globe healing the sick. She is me the dreamer, only better, the direct descendant of all that I was not. She will do everything I had hoped to accomplish in life and more. She will not fall short, cut down by a disease more complicated than life itself. She will grow up brave and strong, a clearheaded and fine woman. I get to watch, dust particles in heaven floating over her head. We have come full circle, my friends.

—*The Red Bench: A Descent And Ascent Into Madness*

it's okay...

to know the love of a good man

I have always felt safest underwater. My fondest memories are childhood summers spent at home with my strong, capable, joyful father sitting in a chair counting laps. He would be happy to just sit, and count well into adulthood. I knew he was there, waiting, whenever I came up for air, lingering a moment too long. Mesmerized by the summer sun, and the light patterns dancing across the blue vinyl. My heart was overflowing with joy, and my soul was full of his liquid love. I can still feel him under the currents, weightless and submerged when the world gets quiet. I can almost reach out and touch his hand, playfully splashing. He's not there, and the chair sits empty. His presence lives in all the good parts of me. Kind, funny, sweet, lovable, worthy, faithful, loyal, and true. He's gone missing when I come up for air, but for one brief moment, in between the inhale and the exhale, I forget. I cried today and could have sworn I felt his hand brush away my tears behind moody purple sunglasses. I will never forget how loved and safe I felt, submerged and surrounded by his unconditional love. Seasons come and go, of this the grown-up girl in me is certain. Find out which season fills you up, and hold on tight, then simply release and gently let go. Surrender, and remember love floats.

acknowledgements

I'd like to thank my mother, Ellen May Hickey Cioffa for knowing precisely when to push and when to pull. I'm grateful for her *smothering, "yes mother"* support. To my brother, Tom, for always being way ahead of the curve and sharing your cool factor. Jack and Terry Hickey, thank you for sharing how you walk through life and the invaluable lessons. To my father for his love and guiding light, you were a king among men. Without him, I would not have known the meaning of profound love.

Kara Moran, thank you for jumping into shark-infested waters, and for patiently waiting for me to catch up. You are my favorite, forever ride or die. Malena Holcomb, thank you for being the sister of my soul, and the healer of my heart. Gianni Ghidini, thank you for your keen observations on life, challenging me to always dig deeper, and the art of patience.

To Sue Cioffa and the girls. Thank you for being omnipresent, no matter my mood however *dramatic.*

My gratitude for their early and forever inspiration goes out to so many trailblazers and fierce females, icons, activists, and breakers of the glass ceiling. I could fill a whole book with your names.

A few heartfelt thank-yous to Julie Davidow, Janie Amoia, Gable Cabrera, Felice Pappas, Amalia Natalio, Dr. Laurie Beth Hickey, Patricia Piazzi, Suzanne Hai, Patricia Nash, Kathleen Grace, Nicole Lyons, Deena Levy, Rebecca Batties, Rachel Thompson, Judith Staff, Dori Owen, Michelle Master, Barb Drozdowich, Bakerview Consulting, and Julie Anderson.

Thank you to Feminine Collective, and BadRedhead Media for previously publishing select poems and essays.

To some amazing stand-up men, Mark Blickley, Ken Metz, Tim Quinn, Patrice Lanquetin and Ralph Brancaccio, thank you for nourishing both the feminine and masculine side.

To all the brave survivors, and fierce mental health advocates using their voices to raise awareness, I stand with you.

To Lupita Lovely, my best girl, and funny furball shadow thank you for loving me colorblind.

To Yosbe Design, C. Streetlights, Beyond Def Publishing and Deena Rae with E-BookBuillders for help getting this book ready for the world.

To the orbs and the power of a beautiful chaotic mind, I thank you for all the mind-blowing colors and feelings that obliterate the dark days.

I am a humanist after all, who happens to be a girl.

about the author

Jacqueline Cioffa was an international model for 17 years and celebrity makeup artist. She is a dog lover, crystal collector, and Stone Crab enthusiast. Author of the riveting memoir, *The Red Bench: A Descent and Ascent into Madness*, and the soul-stirring saga, *The Vast Landscape* and *Georgia Pine*, Jacqueline's work has also been widely featured in numerous literary magazines, and anthologies. She's a storyteller, observer, truth teller, essayist, potty mouth, beauty enthusiast and film lover who's traveled the world. Living with Manic Depression, she believes passionately in using her voice to advocate and inspire others.

Author Site: jacquelinecioffa.com

Made in the USA
Columbia, SC
16 April 2022